SELECTED POEMS / PATRICK KAVANAGH

Edited with an introduction

by Paul Muldoon

WAKE FOREST UNIVERSITY PRESS

Selected Poems

Patrick Kavanagh

First edition

Introduction © Paul Muldoon, 2022
Poems © The Trustees of the Estate of
the late Katherine B. Kavanagh, through the
Jonathan Williams Literary Agency, 2022

For permission, write to
Wake Forest University Press
Post Office Box 7333
Winston-Salem, NC 27109
wfupress.wfu.edu
wfupress@wfu.edu

ISBN 978-1-943667-02-4 (paperback)
ISBN 978-1-943667-03-1 (cloth)
LCCN 2021948558

Design by Crisis
Cover image: Basil Blackshaw
Dromara Landscape, 1953
Copyright © 2022 Artists Rights Society
(ARS), New York / DACS, London
Ulster Museum Collection, BELUM.U2012.3.730

Publication of this book was generously
supported by the Boyle Family Fund.

Contents

Introduction

1

The turnips were a-sowing in the fields around Pettigo
As our train passed through.
A horse-cart stopped near the eye of the railway bridge.

These lines from *Lough Derg* (1942) are archetypical Patrick Kavanagh, combining as they do a matter-of-fact tone with material drawn from the workaday world of rural Ireland. The subject matter of the poem, an account of a pilgrimage to Saint Patrick's Purgatory, rather tellingly connects Kavanagh to both a significant forerunner and a significant heir. The forerunner is William Carleton, author of "The Lough Derg Pilgrim" (1830), and the heir is Seamus Heaney, author of "Station Island" (1984). What's remarkable about the worlds represented by Carleton, Kavanagh, and Heaney is their almost total continuity and consistency. The life of an Irish peasant, like the life of an English, French, or Dutch peasant, would barely change for hundreds of years. In my own case, I watched my father sow turnips in the 1950s using a horse-drawn turnip barrow of the kind Kavanagh's farmer must have been using outside Pettigo. When I first visited Dublin, again in the mid-1950s, the streets were notable less for their automobile traffic than for the huge number of horse-drawn brewery drays delivering Guinness to an eager public.

2

Patrick Kavanagh would have been among the first to line up for a pint of plain in McDaid's of Harry Street, the Dublin literary pub *par excellence*. McDaid's was Kavanagh's home from home in Dublin, the city to which he'd first made his way in 1931 with the sole purpose of meeting his mentor, George William Russell, better known as A. E. The fact that he'd walked the 80 miles from Inniskeen, County Monaghan, where he'd been born in October 1904, gives some indication of Kavanagh's determination. It's also an indicator of the extent to which hardship and privation were the order of the day in the Irish countryside. Kavanagh would not only take hardship and privation in his intellectual stride but they would become the staples of his work. From his first collection, *Ploughman and Other Poems* (1936), through *The Great Hunger* (1942), *A Soul for Sale* (1947), and *Come Dance with Kitty Stobling and Other Poems* (1960) to his *Collected Poems* (1964), he presents a stripped-down version of a spiritual and physical poverty inspired partly by his reading of *The Waste Land* but drawn more significantly from his lived experience of "the stony grey soil of Monaghan." It was in 1939, at the outbreak of World War II, that Kavanagh had left that grey soil and moved full-time to Dublin, the city in which he would die more than 30 years later, on November 30, 1967.

3

"I came to Dublin in 1939," as he puts it in his televised "Self-Portrait" of 1962. "It was the worst mistake of my life. The Hitler war had started. I had my comfortable little holding of watery hills beside the Border … When I came to Dublin in 1939 the Irish Literary affair was still booming. It was the notion that Dublin was a literary metropolis and Ireland, as invented and patented by Yeats, Lady Gregory, and Synge, a spiritual entity." What Kavanagh leaves out, or fails to recognize, is that he himself somehow managed to switch Lady Gregory's grand estate at Gort, County Galway, for a diminutive Monaghan version of that place-name, "Gortin":

> That was the year of the Munich bother. Which
> Was most important? I inclined
> To lose my faith in Ballyrush and Gortin
> Till Homer's ghost came whispering to my mind.
> He said: I made the *Iliad* from such
> A local row. Gods make their own importance.

"Epic" is a poem that sets what we describe as the well-made play of "the Hitler war" against the kitchen sink drama of a boundary dispute between the Duffys and the McCabes, and Kavanagh's agonizing on the relative significance of the two has given license to successive generations of Irish poets in their devotion both to the idea of less being more and the winemaker's regard for the concept of *terroir*, also rather succinctly described by W. H. Auden:

> A poet's hope: to be,
> like some valley cheese,
> local, but prized elsewhere.

This leads me to another, related strand in Kavanagh's work which runs the risk of going unnoticed. In the aforementioned "Self-Portrait," he refers to the fact that "for a number of years I was a film critic. I attended the Irish Film Society shows of a Saturday and wrote as enthusiastically as the next man about the marvelous Italian film — the photography, the direction and the director, a man of superb genius." Though he undercuts this assessment within a sentence or two, saying that he thought most of these foreign films were "poor stuff" — it's telling to me that the date of *The Great Hunger* corresponds precisely with the release of *Quattro passi fra le nuvole* (*Four Steps in the Clouds*), the 1942 Italian comedy-drama film directed by Alessandro Blasetti that is sometimes thought of as the first example of Italian neorealism. I'm not suggesting that Kavanagh is influenced by Blasetti — the dates don't quite add up — but I am suggesting that the neorealist methods of films that used "nonprofessional" actors, shot almost exclusively on location, usually in rundown cities or, in the case of *Quattro passi fra le nuvole*, rundown rural areas, are almost entirely of a piece with the methods of *The Great Hunger*. We recognize here any number of the trademarks of Italian neorealism — the explorations of the conditions of the poor and the lower working class, the characters who exist within a simple social order where survival is the primary objective, the representation of ordinary people performing extraordinarily mundane and quotidian activities that might have been rendered by De Sica or Visconti:

> A dog lying on a torn jacket under a heeled-up cart,
> A horse nosing along the posied headland, trailing
> A rusty plough. Three heads hanging between wide-apart
> Legs. October playing a symphony on a slack wire paling.

All Kavanagh's gifts are on display in these few lines. There's the documentarian's eye and ear for the everyday technical term — "heeled-up," "headland" — used by the likes of my father, born a mere five years later than Kavanagh and a mere 45 miles from Inniskeen. The violent enjambment on "wide-apart / Legs" might seem arbitrary until one remembers that the *jambe* is indeed "a leg." The poem also brings its own musical score, with a matching of sound to picture in the plangent string section. The simple declarative sentences are prosaic in the strictest sense, pushing forward the action and reminding us of Kavanagh's own brilliant forays into prose in *The Green Fool* (1938) and, supremely, *Tarry Flynn* (1948).

4

On an apple-ripe September morning
Through the mist-chill fields I went
With a pitchfork on my shoulder
Less for use than for devilment.

Despite the several local delights in this verse version of *Tarry Flynn* — the nitty-gritty of the "haggard," "drag," the "scraw-knife," and that "pitchfork" — I decided not to include it in this *Selected Poems*. That's partly because, however amusing the image of Kavanagh as a devil with a pitchfork rather than a trident, the poem, also published separately as "Threshing Morning," dissolves into the merely sentimental assertiveness of "And I knew as I entered that I had come / Through fields that were part of no earthly estate." The pitchfork here is no match for the "pitchfork-armed claims" we meet in "Epic":

I have lived in important places, times
When great events were decided: who owned

That half a rood of rock, a no-man's land
Surrounded by our pitchfork-armed claims.
I heard the Duffys shouting 'Damn your soul'
And old McCabe, stripped to the waist, seen
Step the plot defying blue cast-steel —
'Here is the march along these iron stones.'

In *Lough Derg*, the idea of a fight over the precise demarcation of a frontier would have given Kavanagh's reference to "the fields around Pettigo" a little added frisson, particularly since the partition of Ireland in 1922 resulted in the border running down the main street of that village. Conscious though I am of Kavanagh's exaggerated downplaying, if not outright dismissal, of some of his best work, I decided to ignore the fact that *Lough Derg* was not published in his lifetime and include it here. I choose to overlook its occasional *longueurs* in favor of its documentary strengths. All told, I trust this selection of 40 poems will allow Patrick Kavanagh's genius to shine through and represent a beacon of clarity and conciseness by which so many of the rest of us will continue to steer.

PAUL MULDOON, 2022

SELECTED POEMS / PATRICK KAVANAGH

Ploughman

I turn the lea-green down
Gaily now,
And paint the meadow brown
With my plough.

I dream with silvery gull
And brazen crow.
A thing that is beautiful
I may know.

Tranquillity walks with me
And no care.
O, the quiet ecstasy
Like a prayer.

I find a star-lovely art
In a dark sod.
Joy that is timeless! O heart
That knows God!

To a Late Poplar

Not yet half-drest,
O tardy bride!
And the priest
And the bridegroom and the guests
Have been waiting a full hour.

The meadow choir
Is playing the wedding march
Two fields away,
And squirrels are already leaping in ecstasy
Among leaf-full branches.

Tinker's Wife

I saw her amid the dunghill debris
Looking for things
Such as an old pair of shoes or gaiters.
She was a young woman,
A tinker's wife.
Her face had streaks of care
Like wires across it,
But she was supple
As a young goat
On a windy hill.

She searched on the dunghill debris,
Tripping gingerly
Over tin canisters
And sharp-broken
Dinner plates.

Inniskeen Road: July Evening

The bicycles go by in twos and threes —
There's a dance in Billy Brennan's barn tonight,
And there's the half-talk code of mysteries
And the wink-and-elbow language of delight.
Half-past eight and there is not a spot
Upon a mile of road, no shadow thrown
That might turn out a man or woman, not
A footfall tapping secrecies of stone.

I have what every poet hates in spite
Of all the solemn talk of contemplation.
Oh, Alexander Selkirk knew the plight
Of being king and government and nation.
A road, a mile of kingdom, I am king
Of banks and stones and every blooming thing.

Sanctity

To be a poet and not know the trade,
To be a lover and repel all women;
Twin ironies by which great saints are made,
The agonizing pincer-jaws of Heaven.

The Hired Boy

Let me be no wiser than the dull
And leg-dragged boy who wrought
For John Maguire in Donaghmoyne
With never a vain thought
For fortune waiting round the next
Blind turning of Life's lane;
In dreams he never married a lady
To be dreamed-divorced again.

He knew what he wanted to know —
How the best potatoes are grown
And how to put flesh on a York pig's back
And clay on a hilly bone.
And how to be satisfied with the little
The destiny masters give
To the beasts of the tillage country —
To be damned and yet to live.

Shancoduff

My black hills have never seen the sun rising,
Eternally they look north towards Armagh.
Lot's wife would not be salt if she had been
Incurious as my black hills that are happy
When dawn whitens Glassdrummond chapel.

My hills hoard the bright shillings of March
While the sun searches in every pocket.
They are my Alps and I have climbed the Matterhorn
With a sheaf of hay for three perishing calves
In the field under the Big Forth of Rocksavage.

The sleety winds fondle the rushy beards of Shancoduff
While the cattle-drovers sheltering in the Featherna Bush
Look up and say: 'Who owns them hungry hills
That the water-hen and snipe must have forsaken?
A poet? Then by heavens he must be poor.'
I hear and is my heart not badly shaken?

Poplar Memory

I walked under the autumned poplars that my father planted
On a day in April when I was a child
Running beside the heap of suckers
From which he picked the straightest, most promising.

My father dreamt forests, he is dead —
And there are poplar forests in the waste-places
And on the banks of drains.

When I look up
I see my father
Peering through the branched sky.

Pursuit of an Ideal

November is come and I wait for you still,
O nimble-footed nymph who slipped me when
I sighted you among some silly men
And charged you with the power of my will.
Headlong I charged to make a passionate kill,
Too easy, far too easy, I cried then,
You were not worth one drop from off my pen.
O flower of the common light, the thrill
Of common things raised up to angelhood
Leaped in your flirt-wild legs. I followed you
Through April, May and June into September,
And still you kept your lead till passion's food
Went stale within my satchel. Now I woo
The footprints that you make across November.

Memory of My Father

Every old man I see
Reminds me of my father
When he had fallen in love with death
One time when sheaves were gathered.

That man I saw in Gardiner Street
Stumble on the kerb was one,
He stared at me half-eyed,
I might have been his son.

And I remember the musician
Faltering over his fiddle
In Bayswater, London,
He too set me the riddle.

Every old man I see
In October-coloured weather
Seems to say to me:
'I was once your father.'

To the Man After the Harrow

Now leave the check-reins slack,
The seed is flying far today —
The seed like stars against the black
Eternity of April clay.

This seed is potent as the seed
Of knowledge in the Hebrew Book,
So drive your horses in the creed
Of God the Father as a stook.

Forget the men on Brady's hill.
Forget what Brady's boy may say,
For destiny will not fulfil
Unless you let the harrow play.

Forget the worm's opinion too
Of hooves and pointed harrow-pins,
For you are driving your horses through
The mist where Genesis begins.

Spraying the Potatoes

The barrels of blue potato-spray
Stood on a headland of July
Beside an orchard wall where roses
Were young girls hanging from the sky.

The flocks of green potato-stalks
Were blossom spread for sudden flight,
The Kerr's Pinks in a frivelled blue,
The Arran Banners wearing white.

And over that potato-field
A lazy veil of woven sun.
Dandelions growing on headlands, showing
Their unloved hearts to everyone.

And I was there with the knapsack sprayer
On the barrel's edge poised. A wasp was floating
Dead on a sunken briar leaf
Over a copper-poisoned ocean.

The axle-roll of a rut-locked cart
Broke the burnt stick of noon in two.
An old man came through a corn-field
Remembering his youth and some Ruth he knew.

He turned my way. 'God further the work.'
He echoed an ancient farming prayer.
I thanked him. He eyed the potato-drills.
He said: 'You are bound to have good ones there.'

We talked and our talk was a theme of kings,
A theme for strings. He hunkered down
In the shade of the orchard wall. O roses,
The old man dies in the young girl's frown.

And poet lost to potato-fields,
Remembering the lime and copper smell
Of the spraying barrels he is not lost
Or till blossomed stalks cannot weave a spell.

Stony Grey Soil

O stony grey soil of Monaghan,
The laugh from my love you thieved;
You took the gay child of my passion
And gave me your clod-conceived.

You clogged the feet of my boyhood,
And I believed that my stumble
Had the poise and stride of Apollo
And his voice my thick-tongued mumble.

You told me the plough was immortal!
O green-life-conquering plough!
Your mandril strained, your coulter blunted
In the smooth lea-field of my brow.

You sang on steaming dunghills
A song of cowards' brood,
You perfumed my clothes with weasel itch,
You fed me on swinish food.

You flung a ditch on my vision
Of beauty, love and truth.
O stony grey soil of Monaghan,
You burgled my bank of youth!

Lost the long hours of pleasure,
All the women that love young men.
O can I still stroke the monster's back
Or write with unpoisoned pen

His name in these lonely verses,
Or mention the dark fields where
The first gay flight of my lyric
Got caught in a peasant's prayer.

Mullahinsha, Drummeril, Black Shanco —
Wherever I turn I see
In the stony grey soil of Monaghan
Dead loves that were born for me.

A Christmas Childhood

I

One side of the potato-pits was white with frost —
How wonderful that was, how wonderful!
And when we put our ears to the paling-post
The music that came out was magical.

The light between the ricks of hay and straw
Was a hole in Heaven's gable. An apple tree
With its December-glinting fruit we saw —
O you, Eve, were the world that tempted me

To eat the knowledge that grew in clay
And death the germ within it! Now and then
I can remember something of the gay
Garden that was childhood's. Again

The tracks of cattle to a drinking-place,
A green stone lying sideways in a ditch,
Or any common sight, the transfigured face
Of a beauty that the world did not touch.

II

My father played the melodion
Outside at our gate;
There were stars in the morning east
And they danced to his music.

Across the wild bogs his melodion called
To Lennons and Callans.
As I pulled on my trousers in a hurry
I knew some strange thing had happened.

Outside in the cow-house my mother
Made the music of milking;
The light of her stable-lamp was a star
And the frost of Bethlehem made it twinkle.

A water-hen screeched in the bog,
Mass-going feet
Crunched the wafer-ice on the pot-holes,
Somebody wistfully twisted the bellows wheel.

My child poet picked out the letters
On the grey stone,
In silver the wonder of a Christmas townland,
The winking glitter of a frosty dawn.

Cassiopeia was over
Cassidy's hanging hill,
I looked and three whin bushes rode across
The horizon — the Three Wise Kings.

An old man passing said:
'Can't he make it talk —
The melodion.' I hid in the doorway
And tightened the belt of my box-pleated coat.

I nicked six nicks on the door-post
With my penknife's big blade —
There was a little one for cutting tobacco.
And I was six Christmases of age.

My father played the melodion,
My mother milked the cows,
And I had a prayer like a white rose pinned
On the Virgin Mary's blouse.

Art McCooey

I recover now the time I drove
Cart-loads of dung to an outlying farm —
My foreign possessions in Shancoduff —
With the enthusiasm of a man who sees life simply.

The steam rising from the load is still
Warm enough to thaw my frosty fingers.
In Donnybrook in Dublin ten years later
I see that empire now and the empire builder.

Sometimes meeting a neighbour
In country love-enchantment,
The old mare pulls over to the bank and leaves us
To fiddle folly where November dances.

We wove our disappointments and successes
To patterns of a town-bred logic:
'She might have been sick ...' 'No, never before,
A mystery, Pat, and they all appear so modest.'

We exchanged our fool advices back and forth:
'It easily could be their cow was calving,
And sure the rain was desperate that night ...'
Somewhere in the mists a light was laughing.

We played with the frilly edges of reality
While we puffed our cigarettes;
And sometimes Owney Martin's splitting yell
Would knife the dreamer that the land begets.

'I'll see you after Second Mass on Sunday.'
'Right-o, right-o.' The mare moves on again.
A wheel rides over a heap of gravel
And the mare goes skew-ways like a blinded hen.

Down the lane-way of the popular banshees
By Paddy Bradley's; mud to the ankles;
A hare is grazing in Mat Rooney's meadow;
Maggie Byrne is prowling for dead branches.

Ten loads before tea-time. Was that the laughter
Of the evening bursting school?
The sun sinks low and large behind the hills of Cavan,
A stormy-looking sunset. 'Brave and cool.'

Wash out the cart with a bucket of water and a wangel
Of wheaten straw. Jupiter looks down.
Unlearnedly and unreasonably poetry is shaped,
Awkwardly but alive in the unmeasured womb.

The Long Garden

It was the garden of the golden apples,
A long garden between a railway and a road,
In the sow's rooting where the hen scratches
We dipped our fingers in the pockets of God.

In the thistly hedge old boots were flying sandals
By which we travelled through the childhood skies,
Old buckets rusty-holed with half-hung handles
Were drums to play when old men married wives.

The pole that lifted the clothes-line in the middle
Was the flag-pole on a prince's palace when
We looked at it through fingers crossed to riddle
In evening sunlight miracles for men.

It was the garden of the golden apples,
And when the Carrick train went by we knew
That we could never die till something happened,
Like wishing for a fruit that never grew,

Or wanting to be up on Candlefort
Above the village with its shops and mill.
The racing cyclists' gasp-gapped reports
Hinted of pubs where life can drink his fill.

And when the sun went down into Drumcatton
And the New Moon by its little finger swung
From the telegraph wires, we knew how God had happened
And what the blackbird in the whitethorn sang.

It was the garden of the golden apples,
The half-way house where we had stopped a day
Before we took the west road to Drumcatton
Where the sun was always setting on the play.

The Great Hunger

I

Clay is the word and clay is the flesh
Where the potato-gatherers like mechanized scare-crows move
Along the side-fall of the hill — Maguire and his men.
If we watch them an hour is there anything we can prove
Of life as it is broken-backed over the Book
Of Death? Here crows gabble over worms and frogs
And the gulls like old newspapers are blown clear of the hedges, luckily.
Is there some light of imagination in these wet clods?
Or why do we stand here shivering?
                                    Which of these men
Loved the light and the queen
Too long virgin? Yesterday was summer. Who was it promised marriage
    to himself
Before apples were hung from the ceilings for Hallowe'en?
We will wait and watch the tragedy to the last curtain,
Till the last soul passively like a bag of wet clay
Rolls down the side of the hill, diverted by the angles
Where the plough missed or a spade stands, straitening the way.

A dog lying on a torn jacket under a heeled-up cart,
A horse nosing along the posied headland, trailing

A rusty plough. Three heads hanging between wide-apart
Legs. October playing a symphony on a slack wire paling.
Maguire watches the drills flattened out
And the flints that lit a candle for him on a June altar
Flameless. The drills slipped by and the days slipped by
And he trembled his head away and ran free from the world's halter,
And thought himself wiser than any man in the townland
When he laughed over pints of porter
Of how he came free from every net spread
In the gaps of experience. He shook a knowing head
And pretended to his soul
That children are tedious in hurrying fields of April
Where men are spanging across wide furrows,
Lost in the passion that never needs a wife —
The pricks that pricked were the pointed pins of harrows.
Children scream so loud that the crows could bring
The seed of an acre away with crow-rude jeers.
Patrick Maguire, he called his dog and he flung a stone in the air
And hallooed the birds away that were the birds of the years.
Turn over the weedy clods and tease out the tangled skeins.
What is he looking for there?
He thinks it is a potato, but we know better
Than his mud-gloved fingers probe in this insensitive hair.

'Move forward the basket and balance it steady
In this hollow. Pull down the shafts of that cart, Joe,
And straddle the horse,' Maguire calls.

'The wind's over Brannagan's, now that means rain.
Graip up some withered stalks and see that no potato falls
Over the tail-board going down the ruckety pass —
And *that's* a job we'll have to do in December,
Gravel it and build a kerb on the bog-side. Is that Cassidy's ass
Out in my clover? Curse o' God —
Where is that dog?
Never where he's wanted.' Maguire grunts and spits
Through a clay-wattled moustache and stares about him from the height.
His dream changes again like the cloud-swung wind
And he is not so sure now if his mother was right
When she praised the man who made a field his bride.

Watch him, watch him, that man on a hill whose spirit
Is a wet sack flapping about the knees of time.
He lives that his little fields may stay fertile when his own body
Is spread in the bottom of a ditch under two coulters crossed in Christ's
    Name.

He was suspicious in his youth as a rat near strange bread
When girls laughed; when they screamed he knew that meant
The cry of fillies in season. He could not walk
The easy road to his destiny. He dreamt
The innocence of young brambles to hooked treachery.
O the grip, O the grip of irregular fields! No man escapes.
It could not be that back of the hills love was free
And ditches straight.

No monster hand lifted up children and put down apes
As here.

'O God if I had been wiser!'
That was his sigh like the brown breeze in the thistles.
He looks towards his house and haggard. 'O God if I had been wiser!'
But now a crumpled leaf from the whitethorn bushes
Darts like a frightened robin, and the fence
Shows the green of after-grass through a little window,
And he knows that his own heart is calling his mother a liar.
God's truth is life — even the grotesque shapes of its foulest fire.

The horse lifts its head and cranes
Through the whins and stones
To lip late passion in the crawling clover.
In the gap there's a bush weighted with boulders like morality,
The fools of life bleed if they climb over.

The wind leans from Brady's, and the coltsfoot leaves are holed with rust,
Rain fills the cart-tracks and the sole-plate grooves;
A yellow sun reflects in Donaghmoyne
The poignant light in puddles shaped by hooves.

Come with me, Imagination, into this iron house
And we will watch from the doorway the years run back,
And we will know what a peasant's left hand wrote on the page.
Be easy, October. No cackle hen, horse neigh, tree sough, duck quack.

II

Maguire was faithful to death:
He stayed with his mother till she died
At the age of ninety-one.
She stayed too long,
Wife and mother in one.
When she died
The knuckle-bones were cutting the skin of her son's backside
And he was sixty-five.

O he loved his mother
Above all others.
O he loved his ploughs
And he loved his cows
And his happiest dream
Was to clean his arse
With perennial grass
On the bank of some summer stream;
To smoke his pipe
In a sheltered gripe
In the middle of July —
His face in a mist
And two stones in his fist
And an impotent worm on his thigh.

But his passion became a plague
For he grew feeble bringing the vague

Women of his mind to lust nearness,
Once a week at least flesh must make an appearance.

So Maguire got tired
Of the no-target gun fired
And returned to his headlands of carrots and cabbage,
To the fields once again
Where eunuchs can be men
And life is more lousy than savage.

III

Poor Paddy Maguire, a fourteen-hour day
He worked for years. It was he that lit the fire
And boiled the kettle and gave the cows their hay.
His mother, tall, hard as a Protestant spire,
Came down the stairs bare-foot at the kettle-call
And talked to her son sharply: 'Did you let
The hens out, you?' She had a venomous drawl
And a wizened face like moth-eaten leatherette.
Two black cats peeped between the banisters
And gloated over the bacon-fizzling pan.
Outside the window showed tin canisters.
The snipe of Dawn fell like a whirring stone
And Patrick on a headland stood alone.

The pull is on the traces; it is March
And a cold old black wind is blowing from Dundalk.
The twisting sod rolls over on her back —
The virgin screams before the irresistible sock.
No worry on Maguire's mind this day
Except that he forgot to bring his matches.
'Hop back there, Polly, hoy back, woa, wae.'
From every second hill a neighbour watches
With all the sharpened interest of rivalry.
Yet sometimes when the sun comes through a gap
These men know God the Father in a tree:
The Holy Spirit is the rising sap,
And Christ will be the green leaves that will come
At Easter from the sealed and guarded tomb.

Primroses and the unearthly start of ferns
Among the blackthorn shadows in the ditch,
A dead sparrow and an old waistcoat. Maguire learns
As the horses turn slowly round the which is which
Of love and fear and things half born to mind.
He stands between the plough-handles and he sees
At the end of a long furrow his name signed
Among the poets, prostitutes. With all miseries
He is one. Here with the unfortunate
Who for half moments of paradise
Pay out good days and wait and wait
For sunlight-woven cloaks. O to be wise

As Respectability that knows the price of all things
And marks God's truth in pounds and pence and farthings.

IV

April, and no one able to calculate
How far is it to harvest. They put down
The seeds blindly with sensuous groping fingers,
And sensual sleep dreams subtly underground.
Tomorrow is Wednesday — who cares?
'Remember Eileen Farrelly? I was thinking
A man might do a damned sight worse . . .' That voice is blown
Through a hole in a garden wall —
And who was Eileen now cannot be known.

The cattle are out on grass,
The corn is coming up evenly.
The farm folk are hurrying to catch Mass:
Christ will meet them at the end of the world, the slow and speedier.
But the fields say: only Time can bless.

Maguire knelt beside a pillar where he could spit
Without being seen. He turned an old prayer round:
'Jesus, Mary and Joseph pray for us
Now and at the Hour.' Heaven dazzled death.
'Wonder should I cross-plough that turnip-ground.'

The tension broke. The congregation lifted its head
As one man and coughed in unison.
Five hundred hearts were hungry for life —
Who lives in Christ shall never die the death.
And the candle-lit Altar and the flowers
And the pregnant Tabernacle lifted a moment to Prophecy
Out of the clayey hours.
Maguire sprinkled his face with holy water
As the congregation stood up for the Last Gospel.
He rubbed the dust off his knees with his palm, and then
Coughed the prayer phlegm up from his throat and sighed: Amen.

Once one day in June when he was walking
Among his cattle in the Yellow Meadow
He met a girl carrying a basket —
And he was then a young and heated fellow.
Too earnest, too earnest! He rushed beyond the thing
To the unreal. And he saw Sin
Written in letters larger than John Bunyan dreamt of.
For the strangled impulse there is no redemption.
And that girl was gone and he was counting
The dangers in the fields where love ranted.
He was helpless. He saw his cattle
And stroked their flanks in lieu of wife to handle.
He would have changed the circle if he could,
The circle that was the grass track where he ran.
Twenty times a day he ran round the field

And still there was no winning post where the runner is cheered home.
Desperately he broke the tune,
But however he tried always the same melody crept up from the
    background,
The dragging step of a ploughman going home through the guttery
Headlands under an April-watery moon.
Religion, the fields and the fear of the Lord
And Ignorance giving him the coward's blow;
He dare not rise to pluck the fantasies
From the fruited Tree of Life. He bowed his head
And saw a wet weed twined about his toe.

V

Evening at the cross-roads —
Heavy heads nodding out words as wise
As the rumination of cows after milking.
From the ragged road surface a boy picks up
A piece of gravel and stares at it — and then
He flings it across the elm tree on to the railway.
It means nothing,
Not a damn thing.
Somebody is coming over the metal railway bridge
And his hobnailed boots on the arches sound like a gong
Calling men awake. But the bridge is too narrow —
The men lift their heads a moment. That was only John,
So they dream on.

Night in the elms, night in the grass.
O we are too tired to go home yet. Two cyclists pass
Talking loudly of Kitty and Molly —
Horses or women? wisdom or folly?

A door closes on an evicted dog
Where prayers begin in Barney Meegan's kitchen;
Rosie curses the cat between her devotions;
The daughter prays that she may have three wishes —
Health and wealth and love —
From the fairy who is faith or hope or compounds of.

At the cross-roads the crowd had thinned out:
Last words are uttered. There is no tomorrow;
No future but only time stretched for the mowing of the hay
Or putting an axle in the turf-barrow.

Patrick Maguire went home and made cocoa
And broke a chunk off the loaf of wheaten bread;
His mother called down to him to look again
And make sure that the hen-house was locked. His sister grunted in bed,
The sound of a sow taking up a new position.
Pat opened his trousers wide over the ashes
And dreamt himself to lewd sleepiness.
The clock ticked on. Time passes.

VI

Health and wealth and love he too dreamed of in May
As he sat on the railway slope and watched the children of the place
Picking up a primrose here and a daisy there —
They were picking up life's truth singly. But he dreamt of the Absolute
    envased bouquet —
All or nothing. And it was nothing. For God is not all
In one place, complete and labelled like a case in a railway store
Till Hope comes in and takes it on his shoulder —
O Christ, that is what you have done for us:
In a crumb of bread the whole mystery is.

He read the symbol too sharply and turned
From the five simple doors of sense
To the door whose combination lock has puzzled
Philosopher and priest and common dunce.

Men build their heavens as they build their circles
Of friends. God is in the bits and pieces of Everyday —
A kiss here and a laugh again, and sometimes tears,
A pearl necklace round the neck of poverty.

He sat on the railway slope and watched the evening,
Too beautifully perfect to use,
And his three wishes were three stones too sharp to sit on,
Too hard to carve. Three frozen idols of a speechless muse.

VII

'Now go to Mass and pray and confess your sins
And you'll have all the luck,' his mother said.
He listened to the lie that is a woman's screen
Around a conscience when soft thighs are spread.
And all the while she was setting up the lie
She trusted in Nature that never deceives.
But her son took it as the literal truth.
Religion's walls expand to the push of nature. Morality yields
To sense — but not in little tillage fields.

Life went on like that. One summer morning
Again through a hay-field on her way to the shop —
The grass was wet and over-leaned the path —
And Agnes held her skirts sensationally up,
And not because the grass was wet either.
A man was watching her, Patrick Maguire.
She was in love with passion and its weakness
And the wet grass could never cool the fire
That radiated from her unwanted womb
In that country, in that metaphysical land,
Where flesh was a thought more spiritual than music,
Among the stars — out of the reach of the peasant's hand.

Ah, but the priest was one of the people too —
A farmer's son — and surely he knew

The needs of a brother and sister.
Religion could not be a counter-irritant like a blister,
But the certain standard measured and known
By which a man might re-make his soul though all walls were down
And all earth's pedestalled gods thrown.

VIII

Sitting on a wooden gate,
Sitting on a wooden gate,
Sitting on a wooden gate,
He didn't care a damn.
Said whatever came into his head,
Said whatever came into his head,
Said whatever came into his head
And inconsequently sang.
Inconsequently sang,
While his world withered away.
He had a cigarette to smoke and a pound to spend
On drink the next Saturday.
His cattle were fat
And his horses all that
Midsummer grass could make them.
The young women ran wild
And dreamed of a child.
Joy dreams though the fathers might forsake them

But no one would take them,
No one would take them;
No man could ever see
That their skirts had loosed buttons,
Deliberately loosed buttons.
O the men were as blind as could be.
And Patrick Maguire
From his purgatory fire
Called the gods of the Christian to prove
That this twisted skein
Was the necessary pain
And not the rope that was strangling true love.

But sitting on a wooden gate
Sometime in July
When he was thirty-four or -five,
He gloried in the lie:
He made it read the way it should,
He made life read the evil good
While he cursed the ascetic brotherhood
Without knowing why.
Sitting on a wooden gate
All, all alone,
He sang and laughed
Like a man quite daft,
Or like a man on a channel raft
He fantasied forth his groan.

Sitting on a wooden gate,
Sitting on a wooden gate,
Sitting on a wooden gate
He rode in day-dream cars.
He locked his body with his knees
When the gate swung too much in the breeze,
But while he caught high ecstasies
Life slipped between the bars.

IX

He gave himself another year,
Something was bound to happen before then —
The circle would break down
And he would curve the new one to his own will.
A new rhythm is a new life
And in it marriage is hung and money.
He would be a new man walking through unbroken meadows
Of dawn in the year of One.

The poor peasant talking to himself in a stable door —
An ignorant peasant deep in dung.
What can the passers-by think otherwise?
Where is his silver bowl of knowledge hung?
Why should men be asked to believe in a soul
That is only the mark of a hoof in guttery gaps?

A man is what is written on the label.
And the passing world stares but no one stops
To look closer. So back to the growing crops
And the ridges he never loved.
Nobody will ever know how much tortured poetry the pulled weeds on
     the ridge wrote
Before they withered in the July sun,
Nobody will ever read the wild, sprawling, scrawling mad woman's
     signature,
The hysteria and the boredom of the enclosed nun of his thought.
Like the afterbirth of a cow stretched on a branch in the wind,
Life dried in the veins of these women and men:
The grey and grief and unlove,
The bones in the backs of their hands,
And the chapel pressing its low ceiling over them.

Sometimes they did laugh and see the sunlight,
A narrow slice of divine instruction.
Going along the river at the bend of Sunday
The trout played in the pools encouragement
To jump in love though death bait the hook.
And there would be girls sitting on the grass banks of lanes
Stretch-legged and lingering staring –
A man might take one of them if he had the courage.
But 'No' was in every sentence of their story
Except when the public-house came in and shouted its piece.

The yellow buttercups and the bluebells among the whin bushes
On rocks in the middle of ploughing
Was a bright spoke in the wheel
Of the peasant's mill.
The goldfinches on the railway paling were worth looking at —
A man might imagine then
Himself in Brazil and these birds the Birds of Paradise
And the Amazon and the romance traced on the school map lived again.

Talk in evening corners and under trees
Was like an old book found in a king's tomb.
The children gathered round like students and listened
And some of the saga defied the draught in the open tomb
And was not blown.

X

Their intellectual life consisted in reading
Reynolds' News or the *Sunday Dispatch*,
With sometimes an old almanac brought down from the ceiling
Or a school reader brown with the droppings of thatch.
The sporting results or the headlines of war
Was a humbug profound as the highbrow's Arcana.
Pat tried to be wise to the abstraction of all that
But its secret dribbled down his waistcoat like a drink from a strainer.
He wagered a bob each way on the Derby,

He got a straight tip from a man in a shop —
A double from the Guineas it was and thought himself
A master mathematician when one of them came up
And he could explain how much he'd have drawn
On the double if the second leg had followed the first.
He was betting on form and breeding, he claimed,
And the man that did that could never be burst.
After that they went on to the war, and the generals
On both sides were shown to be stupid as hell.
If he'd taken *that* road, they remarked of a Marshal,
He'd have ... O they knew their geography well.
This was their university. Maguire was an undergraduate
Who dreamed from his lowly position of rising
To a professorship like Larry McKenna or Duffy
Or the pig-gelder Nallon whose knowledge was amazing.
'A treble, full multiple odds ... That's flat porter ...
My turnips are destroyed with the blackguardly crows ...
Another one ... No, you're wrong about that thing I was telling you ...
Did you part with your filly, Jack? I heard that you sold her ...'
The students were all savants by the time of pub-close.

XI

A year passed and another hurried after it
And Patrick Maguire was still six months behind life —
His mother six months ahead of it;

His sister straddle-legged across it: —
One leg in hell and the other in heaven
And between the purgatory of middle-aged virginity —
She prayed for release to heaven or hell.
His mother's voice grew thinner like a rust-worn knife
But it cut more venomously as it thinned,
It cut him up the middle till he became more woman than man,
And it cut through to his mind before the end.

Another field whitened in the April air
And the harrows rattled over the seed.
He gathered the loose stones off the ridges carefully
And grumbled to his men to hurry. He looked like a man who could
    give advice
To foolish young fellows. He was forty-seven,
And there was depth in his jaw and his voice was the voice of a great
    cattle-dealer,
A man with whom the fair-green gods break even.
'I think I ploughed that lea the proper depth,
She ought to give a crop if any land gives . . .
Drive slower with the foal-mare, Joe.'
Joe, a young man of imagined wives,
Smiled to himself and answered like a slave:
'You needn't fear or fret.
I'm taking her as easy, as easy as . . .
Easy there, Fanny, easy, pet.'

They loaded the day-scoured implements on the cart
As the shadows of poplars crookened the furrows.
It was the evening, evening. Patrick was forgetting to be lonely
As he used to be in Aprils long ago.
It was the menopause, the misery-pause.

The schoolgirls passed his house laughing every morning
And sometimes they spoke to him familiarly —
He had an idea. Schoolgirls of thirteen
Would see no political intrigue in an old man's friendship.
Love,
The heifer waiting to be nosed by the old bull.
That notion passed too — there was the danger of talk
And jails are narrower than the five-sod ridge
And colder than the black hills facing Armagh in February.
He sinned over the warm ashes again and his crime
The law's long arm could not serve with 'time'.
His face set like an old judge's pose:
Respectability and righteousness,
Stand for no nonsense.
The priest from the altar called Patrick Maguire's name
To hold the collecting box in the chapel door
During all the Sundays of May.
His neighbours envied him his holy rise,
But he walked down from the church with affected indifference
And took the measure of heaven angle-wise.

He still could laugh and sing,
But not the wild laugh or the abandoned harmony now
That called the world to new silliness from the top of a wooden gate
When thirty-five could take the sparrow's bow.
Let us be kind, let us be kind and sympathetic:
Maybe life is not for joking or for finding happiness in —
This tiny light in Oriental Darkness
Looking out chance windows of poetry or prayer.

And the grief and defeat of men like these peasants
Is God's way — maybe — and we must not want too much
To see.
The twisted thread is stronger than the wind-swept fleece.
And in the end who shall rest in truth's high peace?
Or whose is the world now, even now?
O let us kneel where the blind ploughman kneels
And learn to live without despairing
In a mud-walled space —
Illiterate, unknown and unknowing.
Let us kneel where he kneels
And feel what he feels.

One day he saw a daisy and he thought it
Reminded him of his childhood —
He stopped his cart to look at it.
Was there a fairy hiding behind it?

He helped a poor woman whose cow
Had died on her;
He dragged home a drunken man on a winter's night;
And one rare moment he heard the young people playing on the railway
    stile
And he wished them happiness and whatever they most desired from life.

He saw the sunlight and begrudged no man
His share of what the miserly soil and soul
Gives in a season to a ploughman.
And he cried for his own loss one late night on the pillow
And yet thanked the God who had arranged these things.

Was he then a saint?
A Matt Talbot of Monaghan?

His sister Mary Anne spat poison at the children
Who sometimes came to the door selling raffle tickets
For holy funds.
'Get out you little tramps!' she would scream
As she shook to the hens an apronful of crumbs,
But Patrick often put his hand deep down
In his trouser-pocket and fingered out a penny
Or maybe a tobacco-stained caramel.
'You're soft,' said the sister, 'with other people's money;
It's not a bit funny.'

The cards are shuffled and the deck
Laid flat for cutting — 'Tom Malone,
Cut for trump. I think we'll make
This game, the last, a tanner one.
Hearts. Right. I see you're breaking
Your two-year-old. Play quick, Maguire,
The clock there says it's half-past ten —
Kate, throw another sod on that fire.'
One of the card-players laughs and spits
Into the flame across a shoulder.
Outside, a noise like a rat
Among the hen-roosts. The cock crows over
The frosted townland of the night.
Eleven o'clock and still the game
Goes on and the players seem to be
Drunk in an Orient opium den.
Midnight, one o'clock, two.
Somebody's leg has fallen asleep.
'What about home? Maguire, are you
Using your double-tree this week?
Why? do you want it? Play the ace.
There's it, and that's the last card for me.
A wonderful night, we had. Duffy's place
Is very convenient. Is that a ghost or a tree?'
And so they go home with dragging feet
And their voices rumble like laden carts.
And they are happy as the dead or sleeping . . .
I should have led that ace of hearts.

XII

The fields were bleached white,
The wooden tubs full of water
Were white in the winds
That blew through Brannagan's Gap on their way from Siberia;
The cows on the grassless heights
Followed the hay that had wings —
The February fodder that hung itself on the black branches
Of the hilltop hedge.
A man stood beside a potato-pit
And clapped his arms
And pranced on the crisp roots
And shouted to warm himself.
Then he buck-leaped about the potatoes
And scooped them into a basket.
He looked like a bucking suck-calf
Whose spine was being tickled.
Sometimes he stared across the bogs
And sometimes he straightened his back and vaguely whistled
A tune that weakened his spirit
And saddened his terrier dog's.
A neighbour passed with a spade on his shoulder
And Patrick Maguire, bent like a bridge,
Whistled good morning under his oxter,
And the man the other side of the hedge
Champed his spade on the road at his toes

And talked an old sentimentality
While the wind blew under his clothes.

The mother sickened and stayed in bed all day,
Her head hardly dented the pillow, so light and thin it had worn,
But she still enquired after the household affairs.
She held the strings of her children's Punch and Judy, and when a mouth
    opened
It was her truth that the dolls would have spoken
If they hadn't been made of wood and tin —
'Did you open the barn door, Pat, to let the young calves in?'
The priest called to see her every Saturday
And she told him her troubles and fears:
'If Mary Anne was settled I'd die in peace —
I'm getting on in years.'
'You were a good woman,' said the priest,
'And your children will miss you when you're gone.
The likes of you this parish never knew,
I'm sure they'll not forget the work you've done.'
She reached five bony crooks under the tick —
'Five pounds for Masses — won't you say them quick.'
She died one morning in the beginning of May
And a shower of sparrow-notes was the litany for her dying.
The holy water was sprinkled on the bed-clothes
And her children stood around the bed and cried because it was too late
    for crying.
A mother dead! The tired sentiment:

'Mother, Mother' was a shallow pool
Where sorrow hardly could wash its feet . . .
Mary Anne came away from the deathbed and boiled the calves their
    gruel.
O what was I doing when the procession passed?
Where was I looking?
Young women and men
And I might have joined them.
Who bent the coin of my destiny
That it stuck in the slot?
I remember a night we walked
Through the moon of Donaghmoyne,
Four of us seeking adventure —
It was midsummer forty years ago.
Now I know
The moment that gave the turn to my life.
O Christ! I am locked in a stable with pigs and cows for ever.

XIII

The world looks on
And talks of the peasant:
The peasant has no worries;
In his little lyrical fields
He ploughs and sows;
He eats fresh food,

He loves fresh women,
He is his own master;
As it was in the Beginning,
The simpleness of peasant life.
The birds that sing for him are eternal choirs,
Everywhere he walks there are flowers.
His heart is pure,
His mind is clear,
He can talk to God as Moses and Isaiah talked —
The peasant who is only one remove from the beasts he drives.
The travellers stop their cars to gape over the green bank into his fields: —

There is the source from which all cultures rise,
And all religions,
There is the pool in which the poet dips
And the musician.
Without the peasant base civilization must die,
Unless the clay is in the mouth the singer's singing is useless.
The travellers touch the roots of the grass and feel renewed
When they grasp the steering wheels again.
The peasant is the unspoiled child of Prophecy,
The peasant is all virtues — let us salute him without irony —
The peasant ploughman who is half a vegetable,
Who can react to sun and rain and sometimes even
Regret that the Maker of Light had not touched him more intensely,
Brought him up from the sub-soil to an existence
Of conscious joy. He was not born blind.

He is not always blind: sometimes the cataract yields
To sudden stone-falling or the desire to breed.

The girls pass along the roads
And he can remember what man is,
But there is nothing he can do.
Is there nothing he can do?
Is there no escape?
No escape, no escape.

The cows and horses breed,
And the potato-seed
Gives a bud and a root and rots
In the good mother's way with her sons;
The fledged bird is thrown
From the nest — on its own.
But the peasant in his little acres is tied
To a mother's womb by the wind-toughened navel-cord
Like a goat tethered to the stump of a tree —
He circles around and around wondering why it should be.
No crash,
No drama.
That was how his life happened.
No mad hooves galloping in the sky,
But the weak, washy way of true tragedy —
A sick horse nosing around the meadow for a clean place to die.

XIV

We may come out into the October reality, Imagination,
The sleety wind no longer slants to the black hill where Maguire
And his men are now collecting the scattered harness and baskets.
The dog sitting on a wisp of dry stalks
Watches them through the shadows.
'Back in, back in.' One talks to the horse as to a brother.
Maguire himself is patting a potato-pit against the weather —
An old man fondling a new-piled grave:
'Joe, I hope you didn't forget to hide the spade
For there's rogues in the townland. Hide it flat in a furrow.
I think we ought to be finished by tomorrow.'
Their voices through the darkness sound like voices from a cave,
A dull thudding far away, futile, feeble, far away,
First cousins to the ghosts of the townland.

A light stands in a window. Mary Anne
Has the table set and the tea-pot waiting in the ashes.
She goes to the door and listens and then she calls
From the top of the haggard-wall:
'What's keeping you
And the cows to be milked and all the other work there's to do?'
'All right, all right,
We'll not stay here all night.'

Applause, applause,
The curtain falls.

Applause, applause
From the homing carts and the trees
And the bawling cows at the gates.
From the screeching water-hens
And the mill-race heavy with the Lammas floods curving over the weir.
A train at the station blowing off steam
And the hysterical laughter of the defeated everywhere.
Night, and the futile cards are shuffled again.
Maguire spreads his legs over the impotent cinders that wake no
    manhood now
And he hardly looks to see which card is trump.
His sister tightens her legs and her lips and frizzles up
Like the wick of an oil-less lamp.
The curtain falls —
Applause, applause.

Maguire is not afraid of death, the Church will light him a candle
To see his way through the vaults and he'll understand the
Quality of the clay that dribbles over his coffin.
He'll know the names of the roots that climb down to tickle his feet.
And he will feel no different than when he walked through
    Donaghmoyne.
If he stretches out a hand — a wet clod,
If he opens his nostrils — a dungy smell;
If he opens his eyes once in a million years —
Through a crack in the crust of the earth he may see a face nodding in
Or a woman's legs. Shut them again for that sight is sin.

He will hardly remember that life happened to him —
Something was brighter a moment. Somebody sang in the distance.
A procession passed down a mesmerized street.
He remembers names like Easter and Christmas
By the colour his fields were.
Maybe he will be born again, a bird of an angel's conceit
To sing the gospel of life
To a music as flightily tangent
As a tune on an oboe.
And the serious look of the fields will have changed to the leer of a hobo
Swaggering celestially home to his three wishes granted.
Will that be? will that be?
Or is the earth right that laughs, haw haw,
And does not believe
In an unearthly law.
The earth that says:
Patrick Maguire, the old peasant, can neither be damned nor glorified;
The graveyard in which he will lie will be just a deep-drilled potato-field
Where the seed gets no chance to come through
To the fun of the sun.
The tongue in his mouth is the root of a yew.
Silence, silence. The story is done.

He stands in the doorway of his house
A ragged sculpture of the wind,
October creaks the rotted mattress,

The bedposts fall. No hope. No lust.
The hungry fiend
Screams the apocalypse of clay
In every corner of this land.

Lough Derg

From Cavan and from Leitrim and from Mayo,
From all the thin-faced parishes where hills
Are perished noses running peaty water,
They come to Lough Derg to fast and pray and beg
With all the bitterness of nonentities, and the envy
Of the inarticulate when dealing with an artist.
Their hands push closed the doors that God holds open.
Love-sunlit is an enchanter in June's hours
And flowers and light. These to shopkeepers and small lawyers
Are heresies up beauty's sleeve.

The naïve and simple go on pilgrimage too,
Lovers trying to take God's truth for granted . . .
Listen to the chanted
Evening devotions in the limestone church,
For this is Lough Derg, St Patrick's Purgatory.
He came to this island-acre of greenstone once
To be shut of the smug too-faithful. The story
Is different now:
Solicitors praying for cushy jobs,
To be County Registrar or Coroner;
Shopkeepers threatened with sharper rivals

Than any hook-nosed foreigner;
Mothers whose daughters are Final Medicals,
Too heavy-hipped for thinking;
Wives whose husbands have angina pectoris,
Wives whose husbands have taken to drinking.

But there were the sincere as well,
The innocent who feared the hell
Of sin. The girl who had won
A lover and the girl who had none
Were both in trouble,
Trying to encave in the rubble
Of these rocks the Real,
The part that can feel.
And the half-pilgrims too,
They who are the true
Spirit of Ireland, who joke
Through the Death-mask and take
Virgins of heaven or flesh,
Were on Lough Derg Island
Wanting some half-wish.

Over the black waves of the lake trip the last echoes
Of the bell that has shooed through the chapel door
The last pilgrims, like hens to roost.
The sun through Fermanagh's furze fingers
Looks now on the deserted penance rings of stone

Where only John Flood on St Kevin's Bed lingers
With the sexton's heaven-sure stance, the man who knows
The ins and outs of religion . . .
'Hail glorious St Patrick' a girl sings above
The old-man drone of the harmonium.
The rosary is said and Benediction.
The Sacramental sun turns round and 'Holy, Holy, Holy'
The pilgrims cry, striking their breasts in Purgatory.

The same routine and ritual now
As serves for street processions or Congresses
That take all shapes of souls as a living theme
In a novel refuses nothing. No truth oppresses.
Women and men in bare feet turn again
To the iron crosses and the rutted Beds,
Their feet are swollen and their bellies empty —
But something that is Ireland's secret leads
These petty mean people,
For here's the day of a poor soul freed
To a marvellous beauty above its head.
The Castleblayney grocer trapped in the moment's need
Puts out a hand and writes what he cannot read,
A wisdom astonished at every turn
By some angel that writes in the oddest words.
When he will walk again in Muckno Street
He'll hear from the kitchens of fair-day eating houses
In the after-bargain carouses
News from a country beyond the range of birds.

The lake waves caught the concrete stilts of the Basilica
That spread like a bulldog's hind paws. A Leitrim man,
With a face as sad as a flooded hay-field,
Leaned in an angle of the walls with his rosary beads in his hands.

Beside St Brigid's Cross — an ancient relic,
A fragment of the Middle Ages set
Into the modern masonry of the conventional Basilica
Where everything is ordered and correct —
A queue of pilgrims waiting to renounce
The World, the Flesh, the Devil and all his house.

Like young police recruits being measured
Each pilgrim flattened backwards to the wall
And stretched his arms wide
As he cried:
'I renounce the World, the Flesh and the Devil';
Three times they cried out. A country curate
Stared with a curate leer — he was proud.
The booted
Prior passes by ignoring all the crowd.

'I renounce the World,' a young woman cried.
Her breasts stood high in the pagan sun.
'I renounce . . .' an old monk followed. Then a fat lawyer.
They rejected one by one
The music of Time's choir.

A half-pilgrim looked up at the Carrara marbles,
St Patrick wearing an alb with no stitch dropped.
Once he held a shamrock in his hand
But the stem was flawed and it got lost.

St Brigid and the Blessed Virgin flanked
Ireland's national apostle
On the south-west of the island on the gravel-path
Opposite the men's hostel.

Around the island like soldiers quartered round a barrack-yard
There were houses, and a stall where agnisties
And Catholic Truth pamphlets were sold,
And at the pier end, the grey chapel of St Mary's.

The middle of the island looked like the memory
Of some village evicted by the Famine,
Some corner of a field beside a well,
Old stumps of walls where a stunted boortree is growing.
These were the holy cells of saintly men —
O that was the place where Mickey Fehan lived
And the Reillys before they went to America in the Fifties.
No, this is Lough Derg in County Donegal —
So much alike is our historical
And spiritual pattern, a heap
Of stones anywhere is consecrated
By love's terrible need.

On Lough Derg, too, the silver strands
Of the individual sometimes show
Through the fabric of prison anonymity;
One man's private trouble transcending the divinity
Of the prayer-locked multitude,
A vein of humanity that can bleed
Through the thickest hide.
And such a plot unfolds a moment, so —

In a crevice between the houses and the lake
A tall red-headed man of thirty slouches,
A half-pilgrim who hated prayer,
All truth for which St Patrick's Purgatory vouches.
He was a small farmer who was fond of literature
In a country-schoolmaster way.
He skimmed the sentiment of every pool of experience
And talked heresy lightly from distances
Where nothing was terrifyingly Today,
Where he felt he could be safe and say or sin —
But Christ sometimes bleeds in the museum.
It was the first day of his pilgrimage.
He came to Lough Derg to please the superstition
Which says, 'At least the thing can do no harm',
Yet he alone went out with Jesus fishing.

An ex-monk from Dublin, a broad-faced man
With his Franciscan habit sweeping was a pilgrim,

A sad priest staggering in a megrim
Between doubt and vanity's courtesan.
He had fallen once and secretly, no shame
Tainted the young girl's name,
A convent schoolgirl knowing
Nothing of earth sowing.
He took her three times
As in his day-dreams
These things happened.
Three times finds all
The notes of body's madrigal.
'Twas a failing otherwise
Lost him his priestly faculties.

Barefoot in the kitchen
Of John Flood's cottage
Where the girls of Donegal sat, laughing round on stools,
And iron cranes and crooks
Were loaded with black pots,
And holy-looking women kept going in and out of the rooms
As though some man was a-waking . . .
The red-haired man came in
And saw among the loud, cold women one who
Was not a Holy Biddy
With a rat-trap on her diddy,
But something from the unconverted kingdom,
The beauty that has turned

Convention into forests
Where Adam wanders deranged with half a memory;
And red-haired Robert Fitzsimons
Saw Aggie Meegan, and quietly
An angel was turning over the pages of Mankind's history.
He must have her, she was waiting
By the unprotected gable
Of asceticism's granite castle. The masonry's down
And the sun coming in is blood,
The green of trees is lust,
He saw from the unpeopled country into a town.
Let beauty bag or burst,
The sharp points of truth may not be versed
Too smoothly, but the truth must go in as it occurred,
A bulb of light in the shadows of Lough Derg.

The first evening they prayed till nine o'clock
Around the gravel rings, a hundred decades
Of rosaries, until they hardly knew what words meant —
Their own names when they spoke them sounded mysterious.
They knelt and prayed and rose and prayed
And circled the crosses and kissed the stones
Never looking away from the brimstone bitterness
To the little islands of Pan held in the crooked elbow of the lake.
They closed their eyes to Donegal and the white houses
On the slope of the northern hills.

And these pilgrims of a Western reason
Were not pursuing French-hot miracles.
There were hundreds of them tripping one another
Upon the pilgrim way (O God of Truth,
Keep him who tells this story straight,
Let no cheap insincerity shape his mouth).
These men and boys were not led there
By priests of Maynooth or stories of Italy or Spain,
For this is the penance of the poor
Who know what beauty hides in misery
As beggars, fools and eastern fakirs know.

Black tea, dry bread.
Yesterday's pilgrims went upstairs to bed
And as they slept
The vigil in St Patrick's prison was kept
By the others. The Evening Star
Looked into Purgatory whimsically. Night dreams are
Simple and catching as music-hall tunes
Of the Nineties. We'll ramble through the brambles of starry-strange
    Junes.

On a seat beside the women's hostel four men
Sat and talked spare minutes away;
It was like Sunday evening on a country road
Light and gay.
The talk was 'There's a man

Who must be twenty stone weight — a horrid size ...'
'Larry O'Duff ... yes, like a balloon
Or a new tick of chaff ... Lord, did anyone ever see clearer skies?'
'No rain a while yet, Joe,
And the turnips could be doing with a sup, you know.'
And in the women's talk, too, was woven
Such earth to cool the burning brain of Heaven.
On the steps of the church the monks talked
To Robert of art, music, literature.
'Genius is not measured,' he said,
'In prudent feet and inches,
Old Justice burns the work of Raphael —
Justice was God until he saw His Son
Falling in love with earth's fantastic one,
The woman in whose dunghill of emotion
Grow flowers of poetry, music and the old
Kink in the mind; the fascination
Of sin troubled the mind of God
Until He thought of Charity ...
Have you known Charity? Have I?'
Aggie Meegan passed by
To vigil. Robert was puzzled. Where
Grew the germ of this crooked prayer?
The girl was thrilling as joy's despair.

A schoolmaster from Roscommon led
The vigil prayers that night.

'Hail Queen of Heaven' they sang at twelve.
Someone snored near the porch. A bright
Moon sailed in from the County Tyrone
By the water route that he might make
Queer faces in the stained-glassed windows. Why should sun
Have all the fun?
'Our vows of Baptism we again take . . .'
Every Rosary brought the morning nearer.
The schoolmaster looked at his watch and said:
'Out now for a mouthful of fresh air —
A ten-minute break to clear the head.'

It was cold in the rocky draughts between the houses.
Old women tried
To pull bare feet close to their bellies.
Three o'clock rang from the Prior's house clock.
In the hostels pilgrims slept away a three-day fast.

On the cell-wall beside the sycamore tree,
The tree that never knew a bird,
Aggie sat fiddling with her Rosary
And doubting the power of Lough Derg
To save the season's rose of life
With the ponderous fingers of prayer's philosophy.

Robert was a philosopher, a false one
Who ever takes a sledge to swat a fly.

He talked to the girls as a pedant professor
Talking in a university.
The delicate precise immediacy
That sees a flower half a foot away
He could not learn. He spoke to Aggie
Of powers, passions, with the *naïveté*
Of a ploughman. She did not understand —
She only knew that she could hold his hand
If he stood closer. 'Virtue is sublime,'
He said, 'and it is virtue is the frame
Of all love and learning . . .'
'I want to tell you something,' she whispered,
'Because you are different and will know . . .'
'You don't need to tell me anything, you could not,
For your innocence is pure glass that I see through.'
'You'd be surprised,' she smiled. O God, he gasped
To his soul, what could she mean by that?
They watched the lake waves clapping cold hands together
And saw the morning breaking as it breaks
Over a field where a man is watching a calving cow.
New life, new day.
A half-pilgrim saw it as a rabbiter
Poaching in wood sees
Primeval magic among the trees.

The rusty cross of St Patrick had a dozen
Devotees clustered around it at four o'clock.

Bare knees were going round St Brendan's Bed.
A boy was standing like a ballet dancer poised on the rock
Under the belfry; he stared over at Donegal
Where the white houses on the side of the hills
Popped up like mushrooms in September.
The sun was smiling on a thousand hayfields
That hour, and he must have thought Lough Derg
More unreasonable than ordinary stone.
Perhaps it was an iceberg
That he had glanced at on his journey from Japan,
But the iceberg filled a glass of water
And poured it to the honour of the sun.
Lough Derg in the dawn poured rarer cups. Prayer
And fast that makes the sourest drink rare.
Was that St Paul
Riding his ass down a lane in Donegal?
Christ was lately dead,
Men were afraid
With a new fear, the fear
Of love. There was a laugh freed
For ever and for ever. The Apostles' Creed
Was a fireside poem, the talk of the town . . .
They remember a man who has seen Christ in his thorny crown.

John Flood came out and climbed the rock to ring
His bell for six o'clock. He spoke to the pilgrims:
'Was the night fine?'

'Wonderful, wonderful,' they answered, 'not too cold —
Thank God we have the worst part over us.'

The bell brought the sleepers from their cubicles.
Grey-faced boatmen were getting out a boat.
Mass was said. Another day began.
The penance wheel turned round again.
Pilgrims went out in boats, singing
'O Fare Thee Well, Lough Derg' as they waved
Affection to the persecuting stones.

The Prior went with them — suavely, goodily,
Priestly, painfully directing the boats.
They who were left behind
Felt like the wellwishers who keep house when the funeral
Has left for the chapel.

Lough Derg overwhelmed the individual imagination
And the personal tragedy.
Only God thinks of the dying sparrow
In the middle of a war.
The ex-monk, farmer and the girl
Melted in the crowd
Where only God, the poet,
Followed with interest till he found
Their secret, and constructed from
The chaos of its fire
A reasonable document.

A man's the centre of the world,
A man is not an anonymous
Member of the general public.
The Communion of Saints
Is a Communion of individuals.
God the Father is the Father
Of each one of us.

Then there was war, the slang, the contemporary touch,
The ideologies of the daily papers.
They must seem realer, Churchill, Stalin, Hitler,
Than ideas in the contemplative cloister.
The battles where ten thousand men die
Are more significant than a peasant's emotional problem.
But wars will be merely dry bones in histories
And these common people real living creatures in it
On the unwritten spaces between the lines.
A man throws himself prostrate
And God lies down beside him like a woman
Consoling the hysteria of her lover
That sighs his passion emptily:
'The next time, love, you shall faint in me.'

'Don't ask for life,' the monk said.
'If you meet her
Be easy with your affection;
She's a traitor

To those who love too much
As I have done.'
'What have you done?' said Robert,
'That you've come
To St Patrick's Purgatory?'
The monk told his story
Of how he thought that he
Could make reality
Of the romance of the books
That told of Popes,
Men of genius who drew
Wild colours on the flat page. He knew
Now that madness is not knowing
That laws for the mown hay
Will not serve that which is growing.
Through Lough Derg's fast and meditation
He learned the wisdom of his generation.
He was satisfied now his heart
Was free from the coquetry of art.

Something was unknown
To Robert, not long,
For Aggie told him all
That hour as they sat on the wall
Of Brendan's cell:
Birth, bastardy and murder —
He only heard rocks crashing distantly
When John Flood rang the midday bell.

Now the three of them got out of the story altogether
Almost. Now they were not three egotists
But part of the flood of humanity,
Anonymous, never to write or be written.
They vanish among the forests and we see them
Appearing among the trees for seconds.
Lough Derg rolls its caravan before us
And as the pilgrims pass their thoughts are reckoned.
St Patrick was there, that peasant-faced man,
Whose image was embroidered on political banners
In the days of the AOH and John Redmond.
A kindly soft man this Patrick was, like a farmer
To whom no man might be afraid to tell a story
Of bawdy life as it goes in country places.
Was St Patrick like that?
A shamrock in a politician's hat
Yesterday. Today
The sentimentality of an Urban Councillor
Moving an address of welcome to the Cardinal.
All Ireland's Patricks were present on Lough Derg,
All Ireland that froze for want of Europe.

'And who are you?' said the poet speaking to
The old Leitrim man.
He said, 'I can tell you
What I am.
Servant girls bred my servility:

When I stoop
It is my mother's mother's mother's mother
Each one in turn being called in to spread —
"Wider with your legs," the master of the house said.
Domestic servants taken back and front.
That's why I'm servile. It is not the poverty
Of soil in Leitrim that makes me raise my hat
To fools with fifty pounds in a paper bank.
Domestic servants, no one has told
Their generations as it is, as I
Show the cowardice of the man whose mothers were whored
By five generations of capitalist and lord.'

Time passed.
Three boatloads of Dublin's unemployed came in
At three o'clock led by a priest from Thomas Street
To glutton over the peat-filtered water
And sit back drunk when jobs are found
In the Eternal factory where the boss
Himself must punch the clock.

And the day crawled lazily
Along the orbit of Purgatory.

A baker from Rathfriland,
A solicitor from Derry,
A parish priest from Wicklow,

A civil servant from Kerry,
Sat on the patch of grass,
Their stations for the day
Completed — all things arranged,
Nothing in doubt, nothing gone astray.

O the boredom of Purgatory,
Said the poet then,
This piety that hangs like a fool's, unthought,
This certainty in men,
This three days too-goodness,
Too-neighbourly cries,
Temptation to murder
Mediocrities.

The confession boxes in St Mary's chapel hum
And it is evening now. Prose prayers become
Odes and sonnets.
There is a shrine with money heaped upon it
Before Our Lady of Miraculous Succour.

A woman said her litany:
That my husband may get his health
　　We beseech thee hear us
That my son Joseph may pass the Intermediate
　　We beseech thee hear us

That my daughter Eileen may do well at her music
    We beseech thee hear us
That her aunt may remember us in her will
    We beseech thee hear us
That there may be good weather for the hay
    We beseech thee hear us
That my indigestion may be cured
    We beseech thee hear us
O Mother of Perpetual Succour! in temptation
    Be you near us.
And some deep prayers were shaped like sonnets —

O good St Anthony, your poor client asks
That he may have one moment in his arms
The girl I am thinking of this minute —
I'd love her even if she had no farms
Or a four-footed beast in a stable;
Her father is old, doting down the lanes,
There isn't anyone as able
As I am for cocking hay or cleaning drains.
All this that I am is an engine running
Light down the narrow-gauge railway of life.
St Anthony, I ask for Mary Gunning
Of Rathdrumskean to be my wife.
My strength is a skull battering the wall
Where a remand-prisoner is losing his soul.

St Anne, I am a young girl from Castleblayney,
One of a farmer's six grown daughters.
Our little farm, when the season's rainy,
Is putty spread on stones. The surface waters
Soak all the fields of this north-looking townland.
Last year we lost our acre of potatoes;
And my mother with unmarried daughters round her
Is soaked like our soil in savage natures.
She tries to be as kind as any mother
But what can a mother be in such a house
With arguments going on and such a bother
About the half-boiled pots and unmilked cows.
O Patron of the pure woman who lacks a man,
Let me be free I beg of you, St Anne.

O Sacred Heart of Jesus, I ask of you
A job so I can settle down and marry;
I want to live a decent life. And through
The flames of St Patrick's Purgatory
I go offering every stone-bruise, all my hunger;
In the back-room of my penance I am weaving
An inside-shirt for charity. How longer
Must a fifty-shilling-a-week job be day-dreaming?
The dole and empty minds and empty pockets,
Cup Finals seen from the branches of a tree,
Old films that break the eye-balls in their sockets,
A toss-pit. This is life for such as me.

And I know a girl and I know a room to be let
And a job in a builder's yard to be given yet.

I have sinned old; my lust's a running sore
That drains away my strength. Each morning shout:
'Last night will be the last!' At fifty-four
A broken will's a bone that will not knit.
I slip on the loose rubble of remorse
And grasp at tufts of cocksfoot grass that yield,
My belly is a bankrupt's purse.
My mind is a thrice-failed cropping field
Where the missed ridges give out their ecstasy
To weeds that seed through gaps of indiscretion,
Nettles where barley or potatoes should be.
I set my will in Communion and Confession
But still the sore is dribbling blood, and will,
In spite of penance, prayer and canticle.

This was the banal
Beggary that God heard. Was he bored
As men are with the poor? Christ Lord
Hears in the voices of the meanly poor
Homeric utterances, poetry sweeping through.

More pilgrims came that evening
From the pier.
The old ones watched the boats come

And smothered the ridiculous cheer
That breaks, like a hole in pants,
Where the heroic armies advance.

Somebody brought a newspaper
With news of war.
When they lived in Time they knew
What men killed each other for —
Was it something different in the spelling
Of a useless law?

A man under the campanile said:
'Kipper is fish — nice.'
Somebody else talked of Dempsey:
'Greater than Tunney.' Then a girl's voice
Called: 'You'll get cigarettes inside.'

It was six o'clock in the evening.
Robert sat looking over the lake
Seeing the green islands that were his morning hope
And his evening despair.
The sharp knife of Jansen
Cuts all the green branches.
Not sunlight comes in
But the hot-iron sin,
Branding the shame
Of a beast in the Name

Of Christ on the breast
Of a child of the West.
It was this he had read.
All day he was smitten
By this foul legend written
In the fields, in the skies,
In the sanctuaries.
But now the green tree
Of humanity
Was leafing again,
Forgiveness of sin.
A shading hand over
The brow of the lover.

And as the hours of Lough Derg's time
Stretch long enough to hold a generation,
He sat beside her and promised that no word
Of what he knew should ever be heard.
The bell at nine o'clock closed the last station,
The pilgrims kissed goodbye to stone and clay.
The Prior had declared the end of day.

Morning from the hostel windows was like the morning
In some village street after a dance carouse,
Debauchees of Venus and Bacchus
Half-alive stumbling wearily out of a bleary house.
So these pilgrims stumbled below in the sun
Out of God's public-house.

The Mass was said.
Pilgrims smiled at one another:
How good God was,
How much a loving Father!
How wonderful the punishing stones were!
Another hour and the boats will sail
Into the port of Time.
Are you not glad you came?

John Flood stared at the sky
And shook his proud head knowingly.
No storm, nor rain.
The boats are ready to sail.

The monk appears once more,
Not trailing his robe as before,
But different, his pride gone,
Green hope growing where the feet of Pan
Had hoofed the grass.

Lough Derg, St Patrick's Purgatory in Donegal,
Christendom's purge. Heretical
Around the edges: the centre's hard
As the commonsense of a flamboyant bard.
The twentieth century blows across it now,
But deeply it has kept an ancient vow.
It knows the secret of pain —

O moralist, your preaching is in vain
To tell men of the germ in the grain.

All happened on Lough Derg as it is written
In June nineteen forty-two
When the Germans were fighting outside Rostov.
The poet wrote it down as best he knew,
As integral and completed as the emotion
Of men and women cloaking a burning emotion
In the rags of the commonplace will permit him.
He too was one of them. He too denied
The half of him that was his pride
Yet found it waiting, and the half untrue
Of this story is his pride's rhythm.

The turnips were a-sowing in the fields around Pettigo
As our train passed through.
A horse-cart stopped near the eye of the railway bridge.
By Monaghan and Cavan and Dundalk
By Bundoran and by Omagh the pilgrims went;
And three sad people had found the key to the lock
Of God's delight in disillusionment.

Advent

We have tested and tasted too much, lover —
Through a chink too wide there comes in no wonder.
But here in this Advent-darkened room
Where the dry black bread and the sugarless tea
Of penance will charm back the luxury
Of a child's soul, we'll return to Doom
The knowledge we stole but could not use.
And the newness that was in every stale thing
When we looked at it as children: the spirit-shocking
Wonder in a black slanting Ulster hill,
Or the prophetic astonishment in the tedious talking
Of an old fool, will awake for us and bring
You and me to the yard gate to watch the whins
And the bog-holes, cart-tracks, old stables where Time begins.

O after Christmas we'll have no need to go searching
For the difference that sets an old phrase burning —
We'll hear it in the whispered argument of a churning
Or in the streets where the village boys are lurching.
And we'll hear it among simple, decent men, too,
Who barrow dung in gardens under trees,
Wherever life pours ordinary plenty.

Won't we be rich, my love and I, and please
God we shall not ask for reason's payment,
The why of heart-breaking strangeness in dreeping hedges,
Nor analyse God's breath in common statement.
We have thrown into the dust-bin the clay-minted wages
Of pleasure, knowledge and the conscious hour —
And Christ comes with a January flower.

Peace

And sometimes I am sorry when the grass
Is growing over the stones in quiet hollows
And the cocksfoot leans across the rutted cart-pass,
That I am not the voice of country fellows
Who now are standing by some headland talking
Of turnips and potatoes or young corn
Or turf banks stripped for victory.
Here Peace is still hawking
His coloured combs and scarves and beads of horn.

Upon a headland by a whinny hedge
A hare sits looking down a leaf-lapped furrow;
There's an old plough upside-down on a weedy ridge
And someone is shouldering home a saddle-harrow.
Out of that childhood country what fools climb
To fight with tyrants Love and Life and Time?

Pegasus

My soul was an old horse
Offered for sale in twenty fairs.
I offered him to the Church — the buyers
Were little men who feared his unusual airs.
One said: 'Let him remain unbid
In the wind and rain and hunger
Of sin and we will get him —
With the winkers thrown in — for nothing.'

Then the men of State looked at
What I'd brought for sale.
One minister, wondering if
Another horse-body would fit the tail
That he'd kept for sentiment —
The relic of his own soul —
Said, 'I will graze him in lieu of his labour.'
I lent him for a week or more
And he came back a hurdle of bones,
Starved, overworked, in despair.
I nursed him on the roadside grass
To shape him for another fair.

I lowered my price. I stood him where
The broken-winded, spavined stand
And crooked shopkeepers said that he
Might do a season on the land —
But not for high-paid work in towns.
He'd do a tinker, possibly.
I begged, 'O make some offer now,
A soul is a poor man's tragedy.
He'll draw your dungiest cart,' I said,
'Show you short cuts to Mass,
Teach weather lore, at night collect
Bad debts from poor men's grass.'
                    And they would not.

        Where the
Tinkers quarrel I went down
With my horse, my soul.
I cried, 'Who will bid me half a crown?'
From their rowdy bargaining
Not one turned. 'Soul,' I prayed,
'I have hawked you through the world
Of Church and State and meanest trade.
But this evening, halter off,
Never again will it go on.
On the south side of ditches
There is grazing of the sun.
No more haggling with the world . . .'

As I said these words he grew
Wings upon his back. Now I may ride him
Every land my imagination knew.

Memory of Brother Michael

It would never be morning, always evening,
Golden sunset, golden age —
When Shakespeare, Marlowe and Jonson were writing
The future of England page by page,
A nettle-wild grave was Ireland's stage.

It would never be spring, always autumn,
After a harvest always lost,
When Drake was winning seas for England
We sailed in puddles of the past
Chasing the ghost of Brendan's mast.

The seeds among the dust were less than dust,
Dust we sought, decay,
The young sprout rising smothered in it,
Cursed for being in the way —
And the same is true today.

Culture is always something that was,
Something pedants can measure,
Skull of bard, thigh of chief,
Depth of dried-up river.
Shall we be thus for ever?
Shall we be thus for ever?

Bluebells for Love

There will be bluebells growing under the big trees
And you will be there and I will be there in May;
For some other reason we both will have to delay
The evening in Dunshaughlin — to please
Some imagined relation,
So both of us came to walk through that plantation.

We will be interested in the grass,
In an old bucket-hoop, in the ivy that weaves
Green incongruity among dead leaves,
We will put on surprise at carts that pass —
Only sometimes looking sideways at the bluebells in the plantation,
And never frighten them with too wild an exclamation.

We will be wise, we will not let them guess
That we are watching them or they will pose
A mere façade like boys
Caught out in virtue's naturalness.
We will not impose on the bluebells in that plantation
Too much of our desire's adulation.

We will have other loves — or so they'll think;
The primroses or the ferns or the briars,
Or even the rusty paling wires,

Or the violets on the sunless sorrel bank.
Only as an aside the bluebells in the plantation
Will mean a thing to our dark contemplation.

We'll know love little by little, glance by glance.
Ah, the clay under these roots is so brown!
We'll steal from Heaven while God is in the town —
I caught an angel smiling in a chance
Look through the tree-trunks of the plantation
As you and I walked slowly to the station.

Temptation in Harvest

A poplar leaf was spiked upon a thorn
Above the hedge like a flag of surrender
That the year hung out. I was afraid to wonder
At capitulation in a field of corn.
The yellow posies in the headland grass
Paraded up and down in loud apparel;
If I could search their hearts I'd find a moral
For men and women — but I let them pass.
Hope guarantees the poor that they will be
Masters at haw-time when the robins are
Courageous as a crow or water-hen. O see
There someone on an ash tree's limb
Sawing a stick for a post or a drilling-bar!
I wish that I this moment were with him!

I should not have wished, should not have seen how white
The wings of thistle seeds are, and how gay
Amoral Autumn gives her soul away
And every maidenhead without a fight.
I turned to the stubble of the oats,
Knowing that clay could still seduce my heart
After five years of pavements raised to art.

O the devilry of the fields! petals that goats
Have plucked from rose bushes of vanity!
But here! a small blue flower creeping over
On a trailing stem across an inch-wide chasm.
Even here wild gods have set a net for sanity.
Where can I look and not become a lover
Terrified at each recurring spasm?

This time of the year mind worried
About the threshing of the corn and whether
The yellow streaks in the sunset were for fine weather.
The sides of the ricks were letting in; too hurried
We built them to beat the showers that were flying
All day. 'It's raining in Drummeril now,'
We'd speculate, half happy to think how
Flat on the ground a neighbour's stooks were lying.
Each evening combing the ricks like a lover's hair,
Gently combing the butt-ends to run the rain,
Then running to the gate to see if there
Was anybody travelling on the train.
The Man in the Moon has water on the brain!
I love one! but my ricks are more my care.

An old woman whispered from a bush: 'Stand in
The shadow of the ricks until she passes;
You cannot eat what grows upon Parnassus —
And she is going there as sure as sin.'
I saw her turn her head as she went down

The blackberry lane-way, and I knew
In my heart that only what we love is true —
And not what loves us, we should make our own.
I stayed in indecision by the gate,
As Christ in Gethsemane, to guess
Into the morrow and the day after,
And tried to keep from thinking on the fate
Of those whom beauty tickles into laughter
And leaves them on their backs in muddiness.

The air was drugged with Egypt. Could I go
Over the field to the City of the Kings
Where art, music, letters are the real things?
The stones of the street, the sheds, hedges cried, No.
Earth, earth! I dragged my feet off the ground.
Labourers, animals armed with farm tools,
Ringed me. The one open gap had larch poles
Across it now by memory secured and bound.
The flaggers in the swamp were the reserves
Waiting to lift their dim nostalgic arms
The moment I would move. The noise of carts
Softening into haggards wove new charms.
The simplest memory plays upon the nerves
Symphonies that break down what the will asserts.

O Life, forgive me for my sins! I can hear
In the elm by the potato-pits a thrush;
Rain is falling on the Burning Bush

Where God appeared. Why now do I fear
That clear in the sky where the Evening Star is born?
Why does the inconsequential gabble
Of an old man among the hills so trouble
My thoughts this September evening? Now I turn
Away from the ricks, the sheds, the cabbage garden,
The stones of the street, the thrush song in the tree,
The potato-pits, the flaggers in the swamp;
From the country heart that hardly learned to harden,
From the spotlight of an old-fashioned kitchen lamp
I go to follow her who winked at me.

In Memory of My Mother

I do not think of you lying in the wet clay
Of a Monaghan graveyard; I see
You walking down a lane among the poplars
On your way to the station, or happily

Going to second Mass on a summer Sunday —
You meet me and you say:
'Don't forget to see about the cattle — '
Among your earthiest words the angels stray.

And I think of you walking along a headland
Of green oats in June,
So full of repose, so rich with life —
And I see us meeting at the end of a town

On a fair day by accident, after
The bargains are all made and we can walk
Together through the shops and stalls and markets
Free in the oriental streets of thought.

O you are not lying in the wet clay,
For it is a harvest evening now and we
Are piling up the ricks against the moonlight
And you smile up at us — eternally.

On Raglan Road

On Raglan Road on an autumn day I met her first and knew
That her dark hair would weave a snare that I might one day rue;
I saw the danger, yet I walked along the enchanted way,
And I said, let grief be a fallen leaf at the dawning of the day.

On Grafton Street in November we tripped lightly along the ledge
Of the deep ravine where can be seen the worth of passion's pledge,
The Queen of Hearts still making tarts and I not making hay —
O I loved too much and by such, by such, is happiness thrown away.

I gave her gifts of the mind, I gave her the secret sign that's known
To the artists who have known the true gods of sound and stone
And word and tint. I did not stint for I gave her poems to say
With her own name there and her own dark hair like clouds over fields
   of May.

On a quiet street where old ghosts meet I see her walking now
Away from me so hurriedly my reason must allow
That I had wooed not as I should a creature made of clay —
When the angel woos the clay he'd lose his wings at the dawn of day.

Kerr's Ass

We borrowed the loan of Kerr's big ass
To go to Dundalk with butter,
Brought him home the evening before the market
An exile that night in Mucker.

We heeled up the cart before the door,
We took the harness inside —
The straw-stuffed straddle, the broken breeching
With bits of bull-wire tied;

The winkers that had no choke-band,
The collar and the reins . . .
In Ealing Broadway, London Town,
I name their several names

Until a world comes to life —
Morning, the silent bog,
And the god of imagination waking
In a Mucker fog.

Who Killed James Joyce?

Who killed James Joyce?
I, said the commentator,
I killed James Joyce
For my graduation.

What weapon was used
To slay mighty Ulysses?
The weapon that was used
Was a Harvard thesis.

How did you bury Joyce?
In a broadcast Symposium,
That's how we buried Joyce
To a tuneful encomium.

Who carried the coffin out?
Six Dublin codgers
Led into Langham Place
By W. R. Rodgers.

Who said the burial prayers? —
Please do not hurt me —

Joyce was no Protestant,
Surely not Bertie?

Who killed Finnegan?
I, said a Yale-man,
I was the man who made
The corpse for the wake man.

And did you get high marks,
The Ph.D.?
I got the B.Litt.
And my master's degree.

Did you get money
For your Joycean knowledge?
I got a scholarship
To Trinity College.

I made the pilgrimage
In the Bloomsday swelter
From the Martello Tower
To the cabby's shelter.

Innocence

They laughed at one I loved —
The triangular hill that hung
Under the Big Forth. They said
That I was bounded by the whitethorn hedges
Of the little farm and did not know the world.
But I knew that love's doorway to life
Is the same doorway everywhere.

Ashamed of what I loved
I flung her from me and called her a ditch
Although she was smiling at me with violets.

But now I am back in her briary arms;
The dew of an Indian Summer morning lies
On bleached potato-stalks —
What age am I?

I do not know what age I am,
I am no mortal age;
I know nothing of women,
Nothing of cities,
I cannot die
Unless I walk outside these whitethorn hedges.

Epic

I have lived in important places, times
When great events were decided: who owned
That half a rood of rock, a no-man's land
Surrounded by our pitchfork-armed claims.
I heard the Duffys shouting 'Damn your soul'
And old McCabe, stripped to the waist, seen
Step the plot defying blue cast-steel —
'Here is the march along these iron stones'.
That was the year of the Munich bother. Which
Was most important? I inclined
To lose my faith in Ballyrush and Gortin
Till Homer's ghost came whispering to my mind.
He said: I made the *Iliad* from such
A local row. Gods make their own importance.

On Looking into E. V. Rieu's Homer

Like Achilles you had a goddess for mother,
For only the half-god can see
The immortal in things mortal;
The far-frightened surprise in a crow's flight,
Or the moonlight
That stays for ever in a tree.

In stubble fields the ghosts of corn are
The important spirits the imagination heeds.
Nothing dies; there are no empty
Spaces in the cleanest-reaped fields.

It was no human weakness when you flung
Your body prostrate on a cabbage drill —
Heart-broken with Priam for Hector ravaged;
You did not know why you cried,
This was the night he died —
Most wonderful-horrible
October evening among those cabbages.

The intensity that radiated from
The Far Field Rock — you afterwards denied —
Was the half-god seeing his half-brothers
Joking on the fabulous mountain-side.

I Had a Future

O I had a future,
A future.

Gods of the imagination bring back to life
The personality of those streets,
Not any streets
But the streets of nineteen-forty.

Give the quarter-seeing eyes I looked out of,
The animal-remembering mind,
The fog through which I walked towards the mirage
That was my future.

The women I was to meet,
They were nowhere within sight.

And then the pathos of the blind soul,
Who without knowing stands in its own kingdom.

Bring me a small detail
How I felt about money,
Not frantic as later,
There was the future.

Show me the stretcher-bed I slept on
In a room on Drumcondra Road.
Let John Betjeman call for me in a car.

It is summer and the eerie beat
Of madness in Europe trembles the
Wings of the butterflies along the canal.

O I had a future.

If Ever You Go to Dublin Town

If ever you go to Dublin town
In a hundred years or so,
Inquire for me in Baggot Street
And what I was like to know.
O he was a queer one
Fol dol the di do,
He was a queer one
I tell you.

My great-grandmother knew him well,
He asked her to come and call
On him in his flat and she giggled at the thought
Of a young girl's lovely fall.
O he was dangerous
Fol dol the di do,
He was dangerous
I tell you.

On Pembroke Road look out for my ghost
Dishevelled with shoes untied,
Playing through the railings with little children
Whose children have long since died.
O he was a nice man

Fol dol the di do,
He was a nice man
I tell you.

Go into a pub and listen well
If my voice still echoes there,
Ask the men what their grandsires thought
And tell them to answer fair.
O he was eccentric
Fol dol the di do,
He was eccentric
I tell you.

He had the knack of making men feel
As small as they really were
Which meant as great as God had made them
But as males they disliked his air.
O he was a proud one
Fol dol the di do,
He was a proud one
I tell you.

If ever you go to Dublin town
In a hundred years or so,
Sniff for my personality,
Is it vanity's vapour now?
O he was a vain one

Fol dol the di do,
He was a vain one
I tell you.

I saw his name with a hundred others
In a book in the library;
It said he had never fully achieved
His potentiality.
O he was slothful
Fol dol the di do,
He was slothful
I tell you.

He knew that posterity has no use
For anything but the soul,
The lines that speak the passionate heart,
The spirit that lives alone.
O he was a lone one
Fol dol the di do,
Yet he lived happily
I tell you.

On Reading a Book on Common Wild Flowers

O the prickly sow thistle that grew in the hollow of the Near Field.
I used it as a high jump coming home in the evening —
A hurdle race over the puce blossoms of the sow thistles.
Am I late?
Am I tired?
Is my heart sealed
From the ravening passion that will eat it out
Till there is not one pure moment left?

O the greater fleabane that grew at the back of the potato-pit.
I often trampled through it looking for rabbit burrows!
The burnet saxifrage was there in profusion
And the autumn gentian —
I knew them all by eyesight long before I knew their names.
We were in love before we were introduced.

Let me not moralize or have remorse, for these names
Purify a corner of my mind;
I jump over them and rub them with my hands,
And a free moment appears brand new and spacious
Where I may live beyond the reach of desire.

The Hospital

A year ago I fell in love with the functional ward
Of a chest hospital: square cubicles in a row,
Plain concrete, wash basins — an art lover's woe,
Not counting how the fellow in the next bed snored.
But nothing whatever is by love debarred,
The common and banal her heat can know.
The corridor led to a stairway and below
Was the inexhaustible adventure of a gravelled yard.

This is what love does to things: the Rialto Bridge,
The main gate that was bent by a heavy lorry,
The seat at the back of a shed that was a suntrap.
Naming these things is the love-act and its pledge;
For we must record love's mystery without claptrap,
Snatch out of time the passionate transitory.

October

O leafy yellowness you create for me
A world that was and now is poised above time,
I do not need to puzzle out Eternity
As I walk this arboreal street on the edge of a town.
The breeze, too, even the temperature
And pattern of movement, is precisely the same
As broke my heart for youth passing. Now I am sure
Of something. Something will be mine wherever I am.
I want to throw myself on the public street without caring
For anything but the prayering that the earth offers.
It is October over all my life and the light is staring
As it caught me once in a plantation by the fox coverts.
A man is ploughing ground for winter wheat
And my nineteen years weigh heavily on my feet.

Come Dance with Kitty Stobling

No, no, no, I know I was not important as I moved
Through the colourful country, I was but a single
Item in the picture, the namer not the beloved.
O tedious man with whom no gods commingle.
Beauty, who has described beauty? Once upon a time
I had a myth that was a lie but it served:
Trees walking across the crests of hills and my rhyme
Cavorting on mile-high stilts and the unnerved
Crowds looking up with terror in their rational faces.
O dance with Kitty Stobling, I outrageously
Cried out-of-sense to them, while their timorous paces
Stumbled behind Jove's page boy paging me.
I had a very pleasant journey, thank you sincerely
For giving me my madness back, or nearly.

Canal Bank Walk

Leafy-with-love banks and the green waters of the canal
Pouring redemption for me, that I do
The will of God, wallow in the habitual, the banal,
Grow with nature again as before I grew.
The bright stick trapped, the breeze adding a third
Party to the couple kissing on an old seat,
And a bird gathering materials for the nest for the Word,
Eloquently new and abandoned to its delirious beat.
O unworn world enrapture me, encapture me in a web
Of fabulous grass and eternal voices by a beech,
Feed the gaping need of my senses, give me ad lib
To pray unselfconsciously with overflowing speech,
For this soul needs to be honoured with a new dress woven
From green and blue things and arguments that cannot be proven.

Lines Written on a Seat on the Grand Canal, Dublin

'ERECTED TO THE MEMORY OF MRS DERMOD O'BRIEN'

O commemorate me where there is water,
Canal water preferably, so stilly
Greeny at the heart of summer. Brother
Commemorate me thus beautifully
Where by a lock Niagarously roars
The falls for those who sit in the tremendous silence
Of mid-July. No one will speak in prose
Who finds his way to these Parnassian islands.
A swan goes by head low with many apologies,
Fantastic light looks through the eyes of bridges —
And look! a barge comes bringing from Athy
And other far-flung towns mythologies.
O commemorate me with no hero-courageous
Tomb — just a canal-bank seat for the passer-by.

Literary Adventures

I am here in a garage in Monaghan.
It is June and the weather is warm,
Just a little bit cloudy. There's the sun again
Lifting to importance my sixteen acre farm.
There are three swallows' nests in the rafters above me
And the first clutches are already flying.
Spread this news, tell all if you love me,
You who knew that when sick I was never dying
(Nae gane, nae gane, nae frae us torn
But taking a rest like John Jordan).
                                    Other exclusive
News stories that cannot be ignored:
I climbed Woods' Hill and the elusive
Underworld of the grasses could be heard;
John Lennon shouted across the valley.
Then I saw a New June Moon, quite as stunning
As when young we blessed the sight as something holy . . .
Sensational adventure that is only beginning.

For I am taking this evening walk through places
High up among the Six Great Wonders,
The power privileges, the unborn amazes,

The unplundered,
Where man with no meaning blooms
Large in the eyes of his females:
He doesn't project, nor even assumes
The loss of one necessary believer.
It's as simple as that, it's a matter
Of walking with the little gods, the ignored
Who are so seldom asked to write the letter
Containing the word.
O only free gift! no need for Art any more
When Authority whispers like Tyranny at the end of a bar.